V. We adore You, O Christ, and we bless You.
R. Because by Your holy Cross, You have redeemed the world.

Consider how Jesus, after having been scourged and crowned with thorns, was unjustly condemned by Pilate to die on the Cross.

MY Jesus, it was not Pilate, * no, it was my sins that condemned You to die. * I beg You, by the merits of this sorrowful journey, * to assist my soul in its journey toward eternity. * I love You, my beloved Jesus; * I love You more than myself; * I repent with my whole heart for having offended You. * Never permit me to separate myself from You again. * Grant that I may love You always; * and then do with me what You will. *

—*Our Father, Hail Mary, Glory be to the Father, etc.*

At the Cross her station keeping,
Stood the mournful Mother weeping,
Close to Jesus to the last.

2. JESUS CARRIES HIS CROSS

V. We adore You, O Christ, and we bless You.
R. Because by Your holy Cross, You have redeemed the world.

Consider how Jesus, in making this journey with the Cross on His shoulders, thought of us, and for us offered to His Father the death He was about to undergo.

MY beloved Jesus, * I embrace all the tribulations You have destined for me until death. * I beg You, * by the merits of the pain You suffered in carrying Your Cross, * to give me the necessary help * to carry mine with perfect patience and resignation. * I love You, Jesus, my love; * I repent of having offended You. * Never permit me to separate myself from You again. * Grant that I may love You always; * and then do with me what You will. *

—*Our Father, Hail Mary, Glory be to the Father, etc.*

*Through her heart, His sorrow sharing,
All His bitter anguish bearing,
Lo! the piercing sword had passed!*

3. JESUS FALLS THE FIRST TIME

V. We adore You, O Christ, and we bless You.
R. Because by Your holy Cross, You have redeemed the world.

Consider this first fall of Jesus under His Cross. His flesh was torn by the scourges, His head crowned with thorns, and He had lost a great quantity of blood. He was so weakened that He could scarcely walk, and yet He had to carry this great load upon His shoulders. The soldiers struck Him rudely, and thus He fell several times in His journey.

MY beloved Jesus, * it is not the weight of the Cross, but my sins, * which have made You suffer so much pain. * By the merits of this first fall, * deliver me from the misfortune of falling into mortal sin. * I love You, O my Jesus, with my whole heart; * I repent of having offended You. * Never permit me to offend You again. * Grant that I may love You always; * and then do with me what You will. *

—*Our Father, Hail Mary, Glory be to the Father, etc.*

O, how sad, and sore distressed,
Now was she, that Mother Blessed
Of the sole-begotten One.

7

4. JESUS MEETS HIS SORROWFUL MOTHER

V. We adore You, O Christ, and we bless You.
R. Because by Your holy Cross, You have redeemed the world.

Consider the meeting of the Son and the Mother, which took place on this journey. Jesus and Mary looked at each other, and their looks became as so many arrows to wound those hearts which loved each other so tenderly.

MY most loving Jesus, * by the sorrow You experienced in this meeting, * grant me the grace of a truly devoted love for Your most holy Mother. * And you, my Queen, * who were overwhelmed with sorrow, * obtain for me by your intercession a continual remembrance of the Passion of your Son. * I love You, Jesus, my love; * I repent of ever having offended You. * Never permit me to offend You again. * Grant that I may love You always; * and then do with me what You will. *

—*Our Father, Hail Mary, Glory be to the Father, etc.*

Woe-begone, with heart's prostration,
Mother meek, the bitter Passion
Saw she of her glorious Son.

5. SIMON HELPS JESUS TO CARRY THE CROSS

V. We adore You, O Christ, and we bless You.
R. Because by Your holy Cross, You have redeemed the world.

Consider how the Jews, seeing that at each step Jesus from weakness was on the point of expiring, and fearing that He would die on the way, when they wished Him to die the ignominious death of the Cross, constrained Simon the Cyrenian to carry the Cross behind our Lord.

MY beloved Jesus, * I will not refuse the Cross, as the Cyrenian did; * I accept it, I embrace it. * I accept in particular the death You have destined for me; * with all the pains that may accompany it; * I unite it to Your death, I offer it to You. * You have died for love of me; * I will die for love of You, and to please You. * Help me by Your grace. * I love You, Jesus, my love; * I repent of having offended You. * Never permit me to offend You again. * Grant that I may love You always; * and then do with me what You will. *

—*Our Father, Hail Mary, Glory be to the Father, etc.*

Who could mark, from tears refraining,
Christ's dear Mother uncomplaining,
In so great a sorrow bowed!

6. VERONICA WIPES THE FACE OF JESUS

V. We adore You, O Christ, and we bless You.
R. Because by Your holy Cross, You have redeemed the world.

Consider how the holy woman named Veronica, seeing Jesus so afflicted, and His face bathed in sweat and blood, presented Him with a towel, with which He wiped His adorable face, leaving on it the impression of His holy countenance.

MY beloved Jesus, * Your face was beautiful before, * but in this journey it has lost all its beauty, * and wounds and blood have disfigured it. * My soul also was once beautiful, * when it receive Your grace in Baptism; * but I have disfigured it since by my sins; * You alone, my Redeemer, can restore it to its former beauty. * Do this by Your Passion; * O Jesus. * I repent of having offended You. * Never permit me to offend You again. * Grant that I may love You always; * and then do with me what You will. *

—Our Father, Hail Mary, Glory be to the Father, etc.

Who, unmoved, behold her languish,
Underneath His cross of anguish,
'Mid the fierce, unpitying crowd?

7. JESUS FALLS THE SECOND TIME

V. We adore You, O Christ, and we bless You.
R. Because by Your holy Cross, You have redeemed the world.

Consider the second fall of Jesus under the Cross—a fall which renews the pain of all the wounds of the head and members of our afflicted Lord.

MY most gentle Jesus, * how many times You have pardoned me, * and how many times have I fallen again, and begun again to offend You! * By the merits of this new fall, * give me the necessary help to persevere in Your grace until death. * Grant that in all temptations which assail me * I may always commend myself to You. * I love You, Jesus my love, with my whole heart; * I repent of having offended You. * Never permit me to offend You again. * Grant that I may love You always; * and then do with me what You will. *

—Our Father, Hail Mary, Glory be to the Father, etc.

For His people's sins rejected,
She her Jesus, unprotected,
Saw with thorns, with scourges rent.

8. THE WOMEN OF JERUSALEM WEEP OVER JESUS

V. We adore You, O Christ, and we bless You.
R. Because by Your holy Cross, You have redeemed the world.

Consider how those women wept with compassion at seeing Jesus in such a pitiable state, streaming with blood, as He walked along. But Jesus said to them: Weep not for Me, but for your children.

MY Jesus, laden with sorrows, * I weep for the offenses I have committed against You, * because of the pains they have deserved, * and still more because of the displeasure they have caused You, * Who have loved me so much. * It is Your love, more than the fear of hell, * which causes me to weep for my sins. * My Jesus, I love You more than myself; * I repent of having offended You. * Never permit me to offend You again. * Grant that I may love You always; * and then do with me what You will. *

—*Our Father, Hail Mary, Glory be to the Father, etc.*

Saw her Son from judgment taken,
Her belov'd in death forsaken
Till His Spirit forth He sent.

9. JESUS FALLS THE THIRD TIME

V. We adore You, O Christ, and we bless You.
R. Because by Your holy Cross, You have redeemed the world.

Consider the third fall of Jesus Christ. His weakness was extreme, and the cruelty of His executioners excessive, who tried to hasten His steps when He had scarcely strength to move.

MY outraged Jesus, * by the merits of the weakness You suffered in going to Calvary, * give me strength sufficient to conquer all human respect, * and all my wicked passions, * which have led me to despise Your friendship. * I love You, Jesus my love, with my whole heart; * I repent of having offended You. * Never permit me to offend You again. * Grant that I may love You always; * and then do with me what You will. *

—*Our Father, Hail Mary, Glory be to the Father, etc.*

Fount of love and holy sorrow,
Mother, may my spirit borrow
Somewhat of your woe profound.

10. JESUS IS STRIPPED OF HIS GARMENTS

V. We adore You, O Christ, and we bless You.
R. Because by Your holy Cross, You have redeemed the world.

Consider the violence with which the executioners stripped Jesus. His inner garments adhered to His torn flesh, and they dragged them off so roughly that the skin came with them. Compassionate your Savior thus cruelly treated, and say to Him:

MY innocent Jesus, * by the merits of the torment You have felt, * help me to strip myself of all affection to things of earth, * in order that I may place all my love in You, * Who are so worthy of my love. * I love You, Jesus, with my whole heart; * I repent of having offended You. * Never permit me to offend You again. * Grant that I may love You always; * and then do with me what You will. *

—*Our Father, Hail Mary, Glory be to the Father, etc.*

Unto Christ, with pure emotion,
Raise my contrite heart's devotion,
Love to read in every wound.

11. JESUS IS NAILED TO THE CROSS

V. We adore You, O Christ, and we bless You.
R. Because by Your holy Cross, You have redeemed the world.

Consider how Jesus, after being thrown on the Cross, extended His hands, and offered to His Eternal Father the sacrifice of His death for our salvation. These barbarians fastened Him with nails, and then, raising the Cross, allowed Him to die with anguish on this infamous gibbet.

MY Jesus! loaded with contempt, * nail my heart to Your feet, that it may ever remain there, * to love You, and never leave You again. * I love You more than myself; * I repent of having offended You. * Never permit me to offend You again. * Grant that I may love You always; * and then do with me what You will. *

—*Our Father, Hail Mary, Glory be to the Father, etc.*

Those five wounds on Jesus smitten,
Mother! in my heart be written,
Deep as in your own they be.

12. JESUS IS RAISED UPON THE CROSS, AND DIES

V. We adore You, O Christ, and we bless You.
R. Because by Your holy Cross, You have redeemed the world.

Consider how your Jesus, after three hours' Agony on the Cross, consumed at length with anguish, abandons Himself to the weight of His body, bows His head, and dies.

O MY dying Jesus, * I kiss devoutly the Cross on which You died for love of me. * I have merited by my sins to die a miserable death; * but Your death is my hope. * By the merits of Your death, * give me grace to die, embracing Your feet, * and burning with love for You. * I yield my soul into Your hands. * I love You with my whole heart; * I repent of ever having offended You. * Never permit me to offend You again. * Grant that I may love You always; * and then do with me what You will. *

—Our Father, Hail Mary, Glory be to the Father, etc.

You, my Savior's Cross who bear,
And your Son's rebuke who share,
Let me share them both with you!

13. JESUS IS TAKEN DOWN FROM THE CROSS

V. We adore You, O Christ, and we bless You.
R. Because by Your holy Cross, You have redeemed the world.

Consider how, after the death of our Lord, two of His disciples, Joseph and Nicodemus, took Him down from the Cross, and placed Him in the arms of His afflicted Mother, who received Him with unutterable tenderness, and pressed Him to her bosom.

O MOTHER of sorrow, for the love of this Son, * accept me for your servant, and pray to Him for me. * And You, my Redeemer, * since You have died for me, * permit me to love You; * for I wish only You, and nothing more. * I love You, my Jesus, * and I repent of ever having offended You. * Never permit me to offend You again. * Grant that I may love You always; * and then do with me what You will. *

—Our Father, Hail Mary, Glory be to the Father, etc.

In the Passion of my Maker,
Be my sinful soul partaker,
Weep till death, and keep with you.

17

14. JESUS IS LAID IN THE SEPULCHER

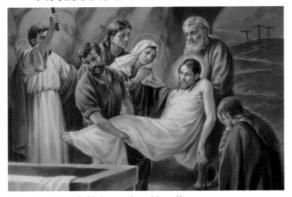

V. We adore You, O Christ, and we bless You.
R. Because by Your holy Cross, You have redeemed the world.

Consider how the disciples carried the body of Jesus to bury it, accompanied by His holy Mother, who arranged it in the sepulcher with her own hands. They then closed the tomb, and all withdrew.

OH, my buried Jesus, * I kiss the stone that encloses You. * But You rose again the third day. * I beg You, by Your resurrection, * make me rise glorious with You at the last day, * to be always united with You in heaven, * to praise You and love You forever. * I love You, and I repent of ever having offended You. * Never permit me to offend You again. * Grant that I may love You always; * and then do with me what You will. *

—*Our Father, Hail Mary, Glory be to the Father, etc.*

Mine with you be that sad station,
There to watch the great Salvation
Wrought upon th' atoning Tree.

After the Stations, say the "Our Father," the "Hail Mary," and the "Glory be to the Father," five times, in honor of the Passion of Jesus Christ, and once for the intention of the Holy Father.

PRAYER TO JESUS CHRIST CRUCIFIED

 BEHOLD, O kind and most sweet Jesus, I cast myself on my knees in Your sight, and with the most fervent desire of my soul, I pray and beg You to impress upon my heart lively sentiments of faith, hope, and charity, with true repentance for my sins, and a firm desire of amendment, while with deep affection and grief of soul I ponder within myself and mentally contemplate Your five most precious Wounds; having before my eyes that which David spoke in prophecy: "They have pierced My hands and My feet; I can count all My bones."

The faithful who, after receiving Communion, recite this prayer before a picture of Christ Crucified may gain a plenary indulgence on any Friday in Lent and a partial indulgence on other days of the year, with the addition of prayers for the Holy Father's intention. (No. 22.)

19

SCRIPTURAL WAY OF THE CROSS[*]

The Way of the Cross is a devotion in which we meditate on Christ's Passion and Death in order to put their meaning into our lives. This Passion and Death are "revelations" of the love of God the Father for all people and of Christ's love for the Father and all people. The devotion of the Way of the Cross should lead us to do in our lives what Jesus did—we must give our lives in the service of others.

OPENING PRAYER

HEAVENLY Father,
grant that we who meditate on the Passion and Death
of Your Son, Jesus Christ,
may imitate in our lives
His love and self-giving to You and to others.
We ask this through Christ our Lord. Amen.

1. JESUS IS CONDEMNED TO DEATH

GOD so loved the world
that He gave His only Son . . .
to save the world through Him (Jn 3:16f).

He was harshly treated, yet He submitted
and did not open His mouth.
He was silent like a lamb led to the slaughter
or a sheep before the shearers,
and did not open His mouth (Isa 53:7).

---

* Reprinted here from the *People's Prayer Book*, which received the Imprimatur from the Vicar General of the Archdiocese of New York, Robert A. Brucato, D.D., in 2001.

No one has greater love than this:
to lay down one's life for one's friends (Jn
    15:13).

Let us pray.
Father,
in the flesh of Your Son
You condemned sin.
Grant us the gift of eternal life
in the same Christ our Lord. Amen.

2. JESUS BEARS HIS CROSS

SURELY, He took up our infirmities
and carried our sorrows (Isa 53:4).

Those who wish to be My followers
must deny their very selves,
take up their cross daily,
and follow Me (Lk 9:23).

Take My yoke upon you and learn from
    Me, . . .
for My yoke is easy and My burden is light (Mt
    11:28f).

Let us pray.
Father,
Your Son Jesus humbled Himself
and became obedient to death.
Teach us to glory above all else in the Cross,

in which is our salvation.
Grant this through Christ our Lord. Amen.

3. JESUS FALLS THE FIRST TIME

HE has broken My teeth with gravel
and trampled Me in the dust.
I have been deprived of peace
and have forgotten what happiness is (Lam 3:16f).

The Lord has laid upon Him the iniquity of us all (Isa 53:6).

Behold the Lamb of God
Who takes away the sin of the world (Jn 1:29).

Let us pray.
Father,
help us to remain irreproachable in Your sight,
so that we can offer You our body
as a holy and living offering.
We ask this in the Name of Jesus the Lord. Amen.

4. JESUS MEETS HIS MOTHER

DID you not know that I must be in My Father's house? (Lk 2:49).

Come, all you who pass by along the road,

look and see
whether there is any pain like My
1:12).

You are now in anguish,
but I will see you again.
Then your hearts will rejoice,
and no one shall deprive you of your joy (Jn
16:22).

Let us pray.
Father,
accept the sorrows of the Blessed Virgin Mary,
Mother of Your Son.
May they obtain from Your mercy
every good for our salvation.
Grant this through Christ our Lord. Amen.

5. JESUS IS HELPED BY SIMON

WHATEVER you did for one
of the least
of these brothers and sisters of
Mine,
you did for Me (Mt 25:40).

Bear one another's burdens,
and in this way you will fulfill the law of Christ
(Gal 6:2).

A servant is not greater than his master (Jn
13:16).

Let us pray.
Father,

You have first loved us
and You sent Your Son to expiate our sins.
Grant that we may love one another
and bear each other's burdens.
We ask this through Christ our Lord. Amen.

6. VERONICA WIPES THE FACE OF JESUS

HIS appearance was disfigured beyond that of any man,
and His form marred beyond any human likeness. (Isa 52:14).

Whoever has seen Me has seen the Father (Jn 14:9).

The Son is the reflection of God's glory and the exact representation of His being (Heb 1:3).

Let us pray.
Heavenly Father,
grant that we may reflect Your Son's glory
and be transformed into His image
so that we may be configured to Him.
We ask this in the Name of Jesus. Amen.

7. JESUS FALLS A SECOND TIME

I WAS hard pressed and close to falling,
but the Lord came to My aid (Ps 118:13).

We do not have a high priest
who is unable to sympathize with our weak-
nesses,
but One Who has been tested in every way as
we are,
but without sinning (Heb 4:15).

Come to Me,
all you who are weary and overburdened,
and I will give you rest (Mt 11:28).

Let us pray.
God our Father,
grant that we may walk in the footsteps of Jesus
Who suffered for us
and redeemed us not with gold and silver
but with the price of His own Blood.
We ask this through Christ our Lord. Amen.

8. JESUS SPEAKS TO THE WOMEN

DAUGHTERS of Jerusalem,
do not weep for Me
but for yourselves and for your
children (Lk 23:28).

Whoever does not abide in Me
will be thrown away like a withered branch (Jn
15:6).

You will all come to the same end
[as some Galileans who perished]
unless you repent (Lk 13:3).

Let us pray.
Heavenly Father,
You desire to show mercy rather than anger
toward all who hope in You.
Grant that we may weep for our sins
and merit the grace of Your glory.
We ask this in the Name of Jesus the Lord.
Amen.

9. JESUS FALLS A THIRD TIME

MY strength is trickling away
like water,
and all My bones are dislocated.
My heart has turned to wax
and melts within Me.
My mouth is as dry as clayware,
and my tongue sticks to My jaws;
You have laid Me down in the dust of death (Ps
22:15f).

Let your attitude be identical to that of Christ: ...
He emptied Himself
taking the form of a slave (Phil 2:5-7).

All who exalt themselves shall be humbled,
and those who humble themselves shall be
exalted (Lk 14:11).

Let us pray.
God our Father,
look with pity on us
oppressed by the weight of our sins
and grant us Your forgiveness.
Help us to serve You with our whole heart.
We ask this through Christ our Lord. Amen.

10. JESUS IS STRIPPED OF HIS GARMENTS

THEY divide My garments among them,
and for My clothing they cast lots (Ps 22:19).

Those who do not renounce all their possessions
cannot be My disciples (Lk 14:33).

Put on the Lord Jesus Christ
and allow no opportunity for the flesh (Rom 13:14).

Let us pray.
Heavenly Father,
let nothing deprive us of Your love—
neither trials nor distress nor persecution.
May we become the wheat of Christ
and be one pure bread.
Grant this through Christ our Lord. Amen.

11. JESUS IS NAILED TO THE CROSS

THEY have pierced My hands and My feet;
I can count all My bones (Ps 22:17f).

Father, forgive them;
they do not know what they are doing (Lk 23:34).

I have come down from heaven
not to do My own Will

but to do the Will of Him Who sent Me (Jn 6:38).

Let us pray.
Heavenly Father,
Your Son reconciled us to You
and to one another.
Help us to embrace His gift of grace
and remain united with You.
We ask this through Christ our Lord. Amen.

12. JESUS DIES ON THE CROSS

WHEN I am lifted up from the earth,
I will draw everyone to Myself (Jn 12:32).

Father, into Your hands I commend My spirit (Lk 23:46).

He humbled Himself
and became obedient to death,
even death on a Cross!
Because of this, God greatly exalted Him (Phil 2:8-9).

Let us pray.
God our Father,
by His Death Your Son has conquered death,
and by His Resurrection He has given us life.
Help us to adore His Death and embrace His Life.
Grant this in the Name of Jesus the Lord. Amen.

13. JESUS IS TAKEN DOWN FROM THE CROSS

THUS it is written that the Messiah would suffer
and on the third day rise from the dead (Lk 24:26).

Those who love Your law have great peace (Ps 119:165).

This is how God showed His love:
He sent His only Son to the world . . .
as an atoning sacrifice for our sins (1 Jn 4:9f).

Let us pray.
God our Father,
grant that we may be associated in Christ's Death
so that we may advance toward the Resurrection
with great hope.
We ask this through Christ our Lord.

14. JESUS IS PLACED IN THE TOMB

UNLESS a grain of wheat falls into the earth and dies,
it remains just a grain of wheat.
However, if it dies,
it bears much fruit (Jn 12:24).

When Christ died, He died to sin, once and for all.

However, the life He lives, He lives for God.
In the same way, you must regard yourselves
as being dead to sin and alive for God
in Christ Jesus (Rom 6:10-11).

Christ . . . was raised to life on the third day
in accordance with the Scriptures (1 Cor 15:4).

Let us pray.
Heavenly Father,
You raised Jesus from the dead
through Your Holy Spirit.
Grant life to our mortal bodies
through that same Spirit Who abides in us.
We ask this in the Name of Jesus the Lord.
       Amen.

CONCLUDING PRAYER

HEAVENLY Father,
You delivered Your Son to the Death of the
  Cross
to save us from evil.
Grant us the grace of the Resurrection.
We ask this through Christ our Lord. Amen.

PRAYER FOR THE GRACE
OF THE PASSION

O LORD,
  for the redemption of the world,
You willed to be born among human beings,